The Deceit of Distraction

Toy Taylor

By Toy Taylor

Printed in the U.S.A

Printed ISBN: 978-1-7335685-8-6

EBOOK ISBN: 978-1-7335685-9-3

Published by: Toy Taylor

Publication: March 2019

ALL RIGHTS RESERVED. NO PORTION of this book may be used without permission of the author, with the exception of brief excerpts for articles, reviews, and etc. No part of this publication may be distributed or transmitted in any form without written permission from the author.

Copies of the books can be ordered online at www.toytaylorbooks.com and through various retailers.

Copyright © 2019 Toy Taylor

I am one grateful Author.

-Toy

He told them their choices and they got upset.

The Deceit of Distractions

Table of Contents

Introduction 13

Chapter 1: Defining Distractions 21

Chapter 2: Spiritual Distractions 35

Chapter 3: Financial Distractions 49

Chapter 4: Relationship Distractions 63

Chapter 5: Mental Distractions 77

Chapter 6: Social Distractions 90

Chapter 7: Manufactured Distractions 103

Chapter 8: The Deceit 116

Chapter 9: The Choice 125

Chapter 10: A Continuum 139

Something You can be Distracted by 152

About the Author 167

Introduction

I hate failure. Who loves it? I have received three failing grades in my academic career. One I received during my undergraduate degree. I received a F in Microeconomics. I deserved that F too.

The next two failing grades I received during my graduate studies. The failing grade during my graduate studies intrigued me the most. I had taught United States history for a year before I began graduate school. I fussed at kids all the time about failing to complete homework. I called parents because of failing grades.

When I asked the kids why they failed to meet grading expectations, they were pretty honest. My male students were "playing the game". This referred to various gaming consoles used to play multiplayer games. One of the most popular games of the time was claiming my students' academic lives.

I felt like asking "you cannot read at your grade level, yet your focus is games?" I was flabbergasted to say the least. Even at the parents who allowed these failing kids to own a console. Come on parents, it is your grade too.

Even worse, this particular game was super violent. I did extensive research on the effects of video games during my undergrad. Game developers put games in the hands of youth that are essentially army training simulators. If America really wants to know why kids are so easily prone to gun violence, just look at games. Kids practice killing religiously.

Then something happened. My boyfriend and I moved in together while I completed graduate school. I told him about this crazy game, and he acknowledge he knew of the game.

He also informed me that he owned the game and the console. It was just at a friend's house since he did not use it much. He asked if I wanted it, of course I took a free console. It was worth hundreds of dollars, even if I did not play it. I could pawn it during hard times.

As promised, his friend delivered the console. It was then regifted to me. I decided to give it a try. I was working on obtaining my principalship certification when I started playing. I was out of school on academic probation by the end of that particular semester.

Now, I submit to you, I gave my students severe tongue lashings for playing the same game. I turned my nose up at parents that allowed their kids to play such games. If your child is failing and they have access to games, my nose is still turned up to you. But if they are passing, play on!

I had failed out of school. I understood it. I got a dose of the Kool-Aid that was enough to separate me from my future. Shortly. I eventually got a grip of myself and caught back up in school. I was awarded my degree as well.

Degree or not, I got distracted. It made me disappointed in myself. I come from a very impoverished background. I stay focused on purpose. I stay focused for my generations that will come after me.

There are many people that come from impoverished backgrounds. Yet, they allow distractions to rule their world as if they have no consideration for time. Distractions are now raising our kids. It shows when you look at academic data.

In 2018, Alexa Lardieri wrote an article for U.S. News reciting some beneficial academic data. She cited the National Academy of Science to back her claims. The Academy had found that United States IQ's have been in decline since 1975. Unlike other academic critics, they did not blame faulty teaching and a poor public-school system. They blamed the child's environment.

This makes the parent just as accountable for their child's intelligence as the teacher. I wish the supporters of standardized testing had this perspective. Instead they blame hard working teachers for distracted students. You would think a parent cared enough about their child to facilitate their academic success. Nope. The ones I have encountered blame a new teacher every year, not their parenting skills.

They are busy being distracted themselves. There are some parents that support their kids and their school community. Then there are most that only contact the school when there is a discrepancy. For example, it takes six weeks to fail a kid on the report card. It is not a one-day decision.

The parent, if they would have checked, could see their kid failing at the third week. Instead, they wait for the failing report card and demand the school performs magic. What does the school do? Oblige the parent. Even I am guilty.

All parties are equally teaching the child it is ok to be irresponsible. Just kick up enough steam and make others fix it at the last minute. Sadly, this is the same kid that cannot hold a job or build a career. I wish I could truly hold kids accountable. Just not at the expense of my career.

The parent is distracted with finances, relationships, and more. Most times, they are rightly so. Sometimes they are not. There are parents out there that spend more time with their friends than their kids. I watch so many kids be dropped off so the parent can "live their best life". It is sickening.

Let me be clear, I plan to live my best life as well. Just not while I have a toddler or elementary student at home needing guidance for their own best life. When parents aren't careful, their distractions are the detriment of their own children. Distractions are deceitful. You don't see their true effect until you are living in it.

Distracted parents are raising distracted children. In return, we have become a distracted society. We are far removed from the fundamental values of living.

Chapter 1: Defining Distractions

According to Webster's Dictionary, a distraction is an object that directs one's attention away from something else. I believe it is a valid definition. Just not valid for this literary piece. It is too broad.

It gives the word "distraction" the ability to take on a positive or negative connotation. It implies that a good thing may be able to distract one from a bad thing. This is true. There are good distractions. Just not for this literary piece right now.

Initially for this literary piece, I will call a distraction anything that equates to an unprofitable task. A distraction can also be anyone that leads one away from or to unprofitable task. My assignment is to point out those distractions that make you stagnant. My goal is to free you from time wasters to achieve your best self.

We all have the ability to achieve our most far-fetched dreams. Few of us will be willing to sacrifice the time it takes to achieve them though. Most people will fail to acknowledge the ability completely. They will remain stagnant until their caskets close.

Some people are comfortable with where they are and what they have. They are aware of their greater self. They are well versed in their capabilities and their potential. Sometimes they even have resources more than available to them as well.

These people have acknowledged their distractions. They realize that there is more to their story than they plan to write. Instead of working diligently for a better future, they willingly pay for their distractions. This compensation can cost them time, money, and many times both.

Like when I chose to play war simulation games instead of study. I knew playing that game would cost me time that had to be made up by retaking classes. I was well aware that that class cost money I would have to pay again. I cut that game on daily despite this knowledge. I was willingly distracted.

There is another distracted person that I am afraid for. This person is not aware they are distracted. For them, being distracted is a lifestyle. They have failed to be exposed to other avenues of living. This type of person most likely inherited their distraction.

This type of distraction is not socially or economically biased. This type of distraction brings tears to the eyes of the rich dad and the poor dad. Let's take a wealthy and middle-class kid for example. The parents work hard to provide the child with advantages not afforded by all.

As the child grows, the lack of struggle erodes the sense of urgency needed to compete successfully in any industry. The parents can work hard to provide opportunities, but the child is more focused on fun at the parent's expense. They fail to possess the self-discipline it takes to maintain a position. The parents then find themselves financially supporting a thirty something year old.

And please, do not be fooled. There are thirty something year olds with homes and cars still begging their parents from handouts. They pay for the distractions they want and beg for the necessities they need. Never understanding they can achieve financial freedom if they put finances over distractions. Even worse, the parents help pay for these distractions instead of raising their kids. The word "no" builds a lot of character by the way.

    I understand why the wealthy and middle-class kids are distracted. To some extent, they can afford to be. Their lack of effort resorts in them going back to a nice home where the bills will be irrefutably paid. They may have to put up with their parent's opinion, but they have a place to sleep and shower.

    What blows my mind is the level of distraction on the impoverished levels. Nothing about poverty felt good to me. That gave me a resilience to get as far away from it as I could. I knew it was more to life, so I went in search of it.

    Yet, I have class mates that were more athletic than me. More intelligent than me.

Even more inclined to be successful than me because of resources and exposure. But they are all still products of poverty till this very day.

Instead of them teaching their kids to focus, plan, and build, they are teaching their kids the latest song and dance moves. They also hang on to false hope of professional athletic contracts and music deals. I wrote in my book Listen Parents, it's Your Grade Too, that more privileged kids go to the league that poor kids. I used cited sources to support my claim. This is not just an opinion.

I pay for entertainment, but not at the expense of my desired future. I cannot wrap my mind around why the impoverish choose those conditions. Before you get all activist on me, I was impoverished. Unless the person has a debilitating handicap or disease, it is a choice. I can go get twenty of my friends to prove it.

On the opposite end of the spectrum, there is a laser focused person achieving their goals. They are not weighed down by profitless task unless by choice. They take advantage of the information and technology available. They use these resources to serve the world and their financial statements.

A popular video streaming company is a good example of this. All users have the freedom to upload their own videos for public view. They also have the right to be a viewer only and never share a single pixel of themselves. Both users have the same rights.

One user uses the company to make money from their uploads. The other watches the uploaded content for free. Same company, but different motives bring different profits or not. I use this example to reveal I am not demonizing any distraction.

My intention is to only point out the unprofitable ones. I use the same aforementioned company for the free distraction. However, it also serves as a free educational tool for me at times. I am not there for fun and giggles all the time.

This leads me to believe, as a self-proclaimed historian, we are living in two ages simultaneously. From one perspective I can call current times The Age of Information. My other vantage point dubs this critical time as an Age of Distractions. A person's repetitive task are indicative of which era they are residing in.

In older times, digital devices were assets of the privileged. The technology originally evolved to make the lives of highly paid professionals more convenient. Like laptops, they were a spin off from the desktop computer. Desktop computers are the spin-off of type writers and so on.

In this context, the technology was being harnessed for the Information Age. Inventors were making professional life accessible outside of the cubicle or office. The goal was widening margins and cutting human capital. Still is.

However, this also meant the technology becoming available to the general public. As technology evolves, devices become obsolete. This condition of obsolete makes it affordable to the masses. They in turn use it for distractions. This makes them apart of the Age of Distractions.

As the devices become more common and accessible, the rate of information exchange has sped up. I noticed this phenomenon while I was completing my undergrad. A popular social media site became available only to college students. I liked it, it was a break away from my hood associates. They plastered mess on the social media sites available to the public.

At first it was calm and college atmosphere like. As soon as my non-college attending friends were granted access, I deactivated my profile. College was an escape from all the drama and trauma one faces in poverty. When that social media site allowed them to bring that distraction back around me, I went stage left.

The same vendettas that were once handled over the phone or in the street, was brought to the internet space. Because I live in the Age of Information, I eventually had to resurface on the internet. A mentor explained to me it was more profitable to seem "real" through these profiles. So, against my will I obliged.

I possess the ability to unfollow people or organizations that post distracting images and information. I can choose to "mute" others and still follow in support. I can interact with others in a more targeted way. All of these luxuries were brought about by technological advancements.

These features further prove my point of people choosing certain circumstances. I see many people that support things that do not profit them. I do as well. Not at the expense of my future. I am not perfect. I make mistakes.

If you are reading this literature, I hope you have an inkling to live in the Information Age. Regardless of your background you can have whatever you are willing to work for. You have to be honest with yourself though. Honest about many things.

One of the first steps you have to take to free yourself from the Deceit of Distractions is identifying your distractions. That requires honesty. Many people do many things to avoid being honest with themselves. They distract themselves on purpose instead of facing their reality.

Many people are not honest with themselves about the time they possess to make their goals happen. Some flat out do not know. They are so stuck in one hypnotic rhythm, they fail to see opportunity in other avenues. I wrote about this in my book Publish 5 Books in 5 Months or Less.

You would be surprised how much time one has when they "trim the fat". Our distractions have so over taken us they feel like a necessity. Ancient history buries us with evidence that humans can survive on less. However, since there is an opportunity to have excess, we take it.

One of my favorite authors Robert Kiyosaki suggests a person should start a part time business while they work their full-time job. When I make this same suggestion to others in casual conversation, they recoil. Many of us are tied up in coworker conversations. Some spend time with long lunches.

There are others that spend time wasting time at work. When we get home, most of us have a decompression ritual that can take two to three hours. I will not even mention kids and their engagements just yet. The last thing most people want to do is start a part time business in their "free" time.

If distractions like "relaxing" and "free time" are not the distraction, it is often fear. Fear is a paralyzing distraction. As you become honest with yourself and make changes, you have to be honest with others. The fear of ostracism will stop a strong man in his tracks.

Keep your mind on your goals. Keep unprofitable opinions out of your mind. Identify your distractions and proactively manage then. You do not have to throw every distraction away. Some you may have to. Others are put away to only achieve specific goals.

Life is waiting to happen to you if you can be honest with yourself and eliminate distractions. Opportunity will present itself once you push past fear and opinions. The only person that will achieve your goals is you. Everyone else is busy achieving their own.

Are you playing or spectating? Are you selling or buying? Are you owning or renting? Are you distracted or achieving? These are all personal questions a person has to be honest with themselves about.

The list of known distractions is as long as infinity. So are the strategies and remedies. Still there are some common ones that everyone wrestles with young, old, Black, White, Hispanic, Christian, Muslim, or Jew. Make a decision to defeat distractions at all cost. You only have an abundant life to gain.

Hard work pays in dividends if the investments are crafted as so. When you are distracted sometimes, you are paying those dividends to others. Do more for yourself than spending time being distracted by others. It is a vital step to success.

Chapter 2: Spiritual Distractions

Spirituality is something most people have in common. Even those that do not acknowledge formal religion. Everyone worships or follows some ideology closely. Everyone recognizes there is a biological thermostat or energy that has to be regulated.

The choice of this regulation is dependent on the person. We can look at depression for example. Depression is an energy, a spirit. It affects the most mentally tough. It discombobulates the weak in mind.

One person may manage depression praying to the God. Another many pray to Buddha. Some may chant to the sun god. Others worship and depend on entities and substances I do not wish to give life.

The point is we all have to regulate our energy and we do this through spirituality. We look for that thing that makes us feel good. I wanted to start with the spirit because I feel like it is our foundation.

You can take all a man's money, if he has the right spirit, he will earn it all back. You can break a woman's heart, she will find another man with the right spirit. A company can fail, a better one will be built if the owner has the right spirit. The spirit is under constant attack from its opposition. The right spirit will rise from all ashes.

My hope is that everyone's spirit is rooted in positivity. I know this is not the truth. No matter their choice, everyone needs to watch for spiritual distractions. The deceit can be spiritually crippling.

The distractions try your faith. They entice you to question your beliefs. Too much indulgence in spiritual distraction will lead one to wearing their oppositions colors. Too little attention to spiritual things that bring you spiritual profit will cause you to lose your foundation.

Spiritual distractions can cause whole populations to be decimated. Let's look at the Holocaust. I believe Hitler was spiritually focused. He was so spiritually focused that he was able to spiritually distract whole countries.

You cannot pay me to believe every soldier acting upon Hitler's will thought they were doing the right thing. Some did, but not all. Somebody in the clan had a positive spiritual belief that taught against killing the innocent. Instead of opposing their spiritual distraction, the gave in to the distraction of fear and ostracism.

Spiritual distractions can be as small as listening to music that contradicts the doctrine you follow. I am guilty of this. I love a good song. The problem is, that good song leads me to another good song. Before I know it, I have heard ten good songs.

As I get older, I realize like distractions separate me from my spiritual Force. No matter what force or spiritual being a person serves, that force has an opposition. Like good and evil. I had to acknowledge that if it is not good, it must be evil. My faith does not accept an in between.

When we put on that lens, life becomes less complicated. The reality is we have on the cloak of pleasure. As a society, if the distraction feels good, we go for it. I emphasize "feels good" because a good thing can come from a bad place.

This is the deceit of a spiritual distraction. If there is a sign that says "serial killers live here" chances are you won't purchase a home in that neighborhood. Unless you are in fact a serial killer. Or you may reside their if you want to be a victim.

Because of this truth, a serial killer has to be stealthier. You would know that they systematically chose and lured their victims if you have ever watched a major crime show. They pretend to be people they are not to gain trust of those they intend to steal life from. They are deceitful.

This is how spiritual distractions operate. They wrap themselves up in self-justification and alluring promises. They do not give you the full story up front. They give you an enticing first sight. By the time you figure out the trick, you are snared.

Spiritual distractions have the power to infect every area of your life if you let them. Everyone is affected by them, but not everyone succumbs to them. I find personally the distractions go for the weakest areas of my life. The personal places where I feel least confident.

If I were a distraction I would too. Why go for a person's most guarded energies? If I were to gnaw at the person's weak points, it will naturally distract their attention from their strong points. A person is like a chain, only as strong as its weakest link.

All the money, cars, and clothes in the world cannot save those who become spiritually distracted. When the wrong energy has distracted a person, the person becomes blind to reasoning. They put away all things that are profitable for them in the name of that spiritual distraction. Outsiders are stunned at the distracted person's actions.

I am going to use good and evil as an example to further explain spiritual distractions. These are two well-known opposing spiritual forces. Both want to distract people away from the other. Their methods of doing so are polar opposite.

One, good, strives to reveal truth. It makes known the outcome of frivolous choices. It grants free will to its abiders to do as they please. It does not actively fight its opposition.

The other is sneaky and stealthy. It dangles carrots to its distracted victims just long enough to get it's will accomplished. It is also satisfied if it passed to another that is susceptible to distraction. It delivers on its promise. It just fails to reveal the detrimental interest that has to be paid until the balance is due.

Two girls from the same neighborhood grow up in the same church. They are both raised with religious values. They both have a workable understanding of right and wrong. Life begins to distract them both at some point.

Let's say it starts in their adolescence. This is when "peer pressure" is at an all-time high. I call peer pressure a spiritual distractions. If the opposing energy can get them distracted enough at this stage, it will have them distracted for life. How do you ask?

Both girls are distracted by guys to have sex. One girl stays focused on her religious teachings. Nothing the guy offers her can persuade her to give up her virginity. She refuses to have sex until she is married. She denies the guy and goes on with her life.

The other girl makes a different decision. The guy offers her financial gifts, public perks, and powerful promises. She has no real way to check the origins of his gains. She has no real evidence he has intentions on fulfilling those promises.

Still, she falls for it anyway. The guy, who is the distraction, get what he wants. He also leaves an unsuspecting gift in her tummy. A child. He neglects to mention this gift as he is enticing her for her virginity.

If she keeps it, she now has a new distraction she is solely responsible for. If she decides not to keep it, she is now haunted by the decision of "what if" and regret. She is also risking infertility. Both options have a lasting mental effect that distracts her in some capacity. If it is not affecting her in a positive way, it is negative.

Failing to avoid her spiritual distraction attacks her finances. Children are expensive. Along with taking care of herself, she will have to concoct a way to keep her child fed. The child also has other non-negotiable needs such as clothing and housing. All of these resources come with a price.

The girl that preserved her virginity will still have other distractions. Her life will not be perfect. No one's life is perfect. Still, that is a major distraction she dodged.

It wrapped itself up like a cute guy. It made promises to bless her. It may indeed bless her. She just needs to be aware of its curses as well. That is the deceit of spiritual distraction.

I have not successfully avoided all spiritual distractions. I try to when I can though. It is a continuous practice. Sometimes the distraction is a person of the same sex looking to antagonize you and steal your positive energy.

The list of spiritual distractions goes on and on. Despite the many spiritual distractions, I have mainly had success with one strategy. I will reveal multiple strategies for other distractions. For this particular one, just one.

The strategy is simple. I focus. I focus on the teachings of my religion. I focus on the past successes to remind myself what God has done for me. I focus proactively.

I try to continuously keep myself inundated with my faith. If I wait until the distraction comes, I will be more inclined to follow it's perfumed scent. If I am filled with my faith, I have less room for the distracting scent. I have more ammunition to withstand the opposition.

My goal here is not to persuade anyone to buy in to a religion. My intention is to make my readers aware of ways distractions will try their spiritual fortitude. Distractions are energy thieves. They want your energy to make their agenda expand.

You just might not be aware of that agenda until you are embedded in it. To avoid this phenomenon, stay focused. Staying focused on your spiritual guidance makes you sensitive to what it is and what it is not. Some distractions are so deceitful you almost need a spiritual X-ray to see their true intentions.

As a human, you will naturally get spiritually distracted. That distraction will take the form of a pot hole at first. It will make you stumble a bit on your spiritual journey. This is a good place to recalibrate spiritually and focus up.

Failing to focus up will cause it to take the form of a ditch. A ditch is bigger than a pothole. It also takes more effort to get out of. Still, getting out is possible.

Next, that ditch evolves into a pit. Problem with the pit is, you cannot see the world above you. You can peer out of the ditch. You are blind so to speak in the pit, only hearing the rest of the world that exist.

I have seen extraordinary stories of people that go from extreme poverty to extreme wealth because they were able to come out of their personal pits of distraction. I know some that will not acknowledge the pit or the distraction that put them there. These people live in extremely dire conditions. They make no real effort to change their circumstances. They accept the product of their distraction as life going forward.

Spiritual distraction has taken this person and dropped them in an abyss. It would take a strong desire and dire discontent with their current situation to save them from the plunge. Both of those requirements are a personal choice. Just like the initial decision to be distracted by the pothole.

Aristotle said, "we are what we repeatedly do." Since I am Christian, I should be repeatedly focusing on Christianity. When the distraction comes, my knowledge will supersede it's deceit. This is the same for all religions and ideologies. Guarding your spirit from distractions is an on-going process.

Failing to do so can cause a person to lose themselves. They are even running the risk of losing their future. Spiritual distractions are meant to break down your energy. Be stronger than spiritual distractions.

Chapter 3: Financial Distractions

Ahhh.. Finances. Dollars. Cash. Mula. Dough. The Bag. Dinero. Yen. Pound. Crypto currency. One of these words resonates with everyone in some shape form or fashion. No matter if you are wealthy, comfortable, or in poverty, money is a common denominator. It is just the use or lack of that creates factions amongst people.

Time has taught me that the wealthy talk about finances freely depending on the crowd. They talk about it more than they spend it. I do not mean bragging about what they have or can afford either. They have constructive talks about how to build and maintain wealth. They discuss more money than they spend.

They devise ways to accumulate more wealth through profitable task. These tasks are formally known as investments. They pay experts to strategize and manage their wealth responsibly. Unprofitable debt makes them itch.

The impoverished do the exact opposite. They spend more money than they discuss. They in fact do brag about what they have and can acquire. This is in hopes to impress the listener or make them feel inferior. Most of the impoverished people that discuss money matters would not know a millionaire if they were sitting next to one.

Instead of making plans to eradicate themselves from poverty, the impoverished dig themselves into deeper financial holes. They make purchases for aesthetic purposes only. They spend with no regard for their tomorrow or retirement. Their consumer debt climbs with their age. They repeatedly buy items to feel good instead of doing better.

Both parties are financially distracted. One is distracted by the building of wealth. The other is distracted by the accumulation of things. One is positive, and one is negative. As I said in Chapter One, the word distraction has the power to have a positive or negative connotation.

My concern is the negative financial distraction. Clearly the financially positive distractions have a profitable purpose. I am currently stuck in the middle. I have purposeful discussions about money. I also spend frivolously on distractions.

If I look at my life, my own in the middleness financially is a reflection of in the middle choices. I am unprofitably distracted sometimes. Other times I am engaged in task that build my future. So, I have one foot in the bank and the other at my favorite food spot. That is my biggest distraction; food.

Before being in the middle, I lived in poverty. My thought, actions, and decisions reflected my dysfunctional environment. No one taught me the meaning or profitable uses of money. It was not until my late twenties that I was exposed to these concepts. My goal now is to eliminate the distractions that keep me from true wealth.

However, do not be fooled. The wealthy can be just as distracted by money as the impoverished. The level of their distractions supersedes those in poverty because of their access to resources. Their resources are more elastic because of their finances. A deceitful distraction can leave a rich man broke.

There is a myriad of examples I can give to paint this picture. Let's start with a person who inherits or receives sudden wealth. Who they are will be magnified by the money. Whatever habits they partake in will have control over their new wealth. If they were not wealthy before, it is probably because they were financially distracted.

The wealth will only enhance their access to their distractions. Their impoverished mindset causes them to spend haphazardly. They give back to all they think they owe. They also give to those they do not even know for show.

The biggest mistake a distracted wealthy person makes is accumulating more liabilities than assets. As the money runs dry, the bills pile high, and the once rich man finds himself back where he started. All the money he lends and gives is not returned during his time of need. Most of the people he assisted are still in need when he needs a hand.

This person was so distracted by what money could buy, they failed to harness it's real power. The goal of money should be to multiply. This is easier said than done when you factor in all the shiny adult toys like cars, homes, and jewelry. I am still working on this goal myself.

Proper planning prevents such scenarios. A sound financial education would have made that wealth propel for generations. Instead it was squandered. A few distractions can cause major loss. A lack of focus will leave the most pretentious humbled.

The impoverished are on the other end of the spectrum. They are enticed by what others can buy. They watch aimlessly as others live their lives. They naturally want the things deemed as "rich". It is a normal human emotion to want better. Who wants worse? Whoever wants worse, they are a nut case.

They wait for the opportunity to have residual funds. Once acquired, they go directly for the item or it's best representation. They take no regard for their future or their offspring's future. They essentially pay for costumes to put on a show.

I have been on this end of the spectrum. I have taken this very road. At some point I realized it was an unprofitable pattern. You buy the material item, your get the attention, and then it is over.

What is not over is the poverty. The anxiety of obtaining the cash for the purchase is one burden. Purchasing the item and hoping it induces the effect I was looking for was another. Wondering what people really thought afterward was another unprofitable distraction.

Then, to top it off, the pain and disparity of over poverty still lingers. Even with the new material item purchased in the home. I did not like that hypnotic rhythm. It was deceitful.

I am afraid to reveal to you that letting go of the cycle is even worse. I understand why some stay in the cycle. Letting go of opinions takes courage. Especially if you were fighting for opinions previously. It is an internal battle that is publicly analyzed. You go from "putting on" to "falling off".

Despite the bad news, I am also here to tell you there is nothing wrong with falling off if it is for a good purpose. It is better to pass up a financial distraction than be tied down by a financial burden. Let them nails go girl, you have kids that need college tuition. Forget that luxury car man, your family has to eat.

I say that so openly because it should be said. There are some people that do not wait for residual funds. They will spend what they have and beg for what they need. Eviction is not just limited to natural hardships. There are people that will spend money on drugs, cloths, and cars instead of paying their rent.

The real crafty ones know how to get what they want, plus have the government and organizations responsible for their living expenses. There is a hard-working impoverished person. They are doing the best they can with the information they have.

My words are not to wound them. When I am financially able, I will help them.

There is a population of able-bodied Americans living fully off the system on purpose. They use it as a "easy road". They are intelligent enough to run enterprises under the table. The whole while, they are accepting government assistance on top of the table as a life incentive.

The middle class may be the worse of the two. We have enough knowledge to save, but not enough discipline to invest. We know how to keep a job, but not a profitable budget. Our credit is good enough to purchase more than the impoverished. However, it is too low to compete with the wealthy.

We are in a cycle of buying now and paying later. Most do not realize their folly until their retirement years. By this time, inflation and physical ability has made their once sound plan obsolete. They are stuck essentially depending on the government and loved ones. Just like the impoverished.

I picked this truth up from reading Robert Kiyosaki books. As I grow older and observe the realities of those on paths I once aspired to be, I live the truth. I just wonder are they aware. I only have control over me, so to each his own.

As I get older, I see the folly in my decisions and do my best to correct them. But, as I get older, the distractions become more ambivalent. Things will present themselves as something you love, the reality is it morphs into something you do not. Oh, the deceit of distractions.

Many people pay significant amounts of money just to realize they do not want what they wanted. Distractions lure us into financially committing to things that bring us no profit. After the price is paid, we are left with a thing and no progress. Just like spiritual distractions, being proactive can prevent this.

As I get older, I become more honest with myself. There are certain areas that require focus to achieve success. Everything else is pretty much a distraction. The trick is separating the good distractions from the unprofitable ones.

One area is education. I do not mean a formal one. Just an education. It can be a degreed education. It can be an acquired or experiential education. I profit from them both.

I used my degreed education to obtain income in the education industry. I use my acquired education to run my hair company. I did not go to business school, but I own a business. The irony.

As I professionally grow, I continuously pay for my education. The more I know, the more potential I have to earn. I deem education profitable formal or not. It has opened doors for me not afforded to those without it.

I saw the value in investing the more educated I became. I was manually investing time and effort and seeing a return in my education. This made it easier to apprehend the concept for other industries.

Education takes time. Education requires accurate research to gain the desired result. Education is a process that leads to profitable returns of managed correctly. This is the concept of investing.

After hearing, seeing, and understanding the concept of investing, I became adamant about my financial investments. Financial investments are the kryptonite for financial distractions. When you are laser focused on investments, you have no time for distractions. You acknowledge that distractions hinder your investments.

Retirement is another subject I give my attention to. Who wants to work until the casket closes? I would think no one. Yet, millions of people spend money they do not have as if they will not get old. I wrote in my book Builder's Code literally, "You will get old."

I wrote this because I see so many operating as if they are not planning to retire. I have friends that are in the club so much the time would have equated to a degree. Instead of seeing the folly and making a profitable decision, they are still going to the club. They claim to have no time for school.

I realized my efforts to explain this concept to them was a distraction. I love them. I wish them the best. However, anyone with a burning desire to have more does not have to be told how. They will search actively and independently for the answer.

I allow them to be distracted financially. It is a choice. I have to minimize my own distractions. Telling unmotivated grown people what to do is a financial and relationship distraction.

I could be giving that time to a more profitable task. I could be focused on building a better future rather than dishing out unsolicited advice. I am here for who wants the profitable truth. The rest of my finances have to stay focused on my time, investments, and retirements.

Chapter 4: Relationship Distractions

Relationship distractions are a very broad issue. Like spiritual distractions, relationship distractions affect a multitude of other components if not managed. Relationship distractions can affect children, careers, and marriages. They cause mental disruptions. They can be the detriment of one's bank account.

For this literary work we will examine selfish distractions. This will dilute the variety of possibilities. It will help you stay focused on the purpose of this book. To become a better, you. If I reveal every relationship distraction I can think of, you will drift to analyzing others and their actions.

Cheating. I want to get right into it. Cheating has to be the most selfish and dangerous relationship distractions. I call it selfish because there are other options. I call it dangerous because it can cause death. That death can be by person or STD, yet people still do it all the time.

I was a cheater. My opinion is women cheat better than men. I am passing no judgments. I just have not cheated on the person I am currently with. Mostly because of the dangerous part.

Cheating is fun and exciting. It gives the participants an adrenaline rush sneaking around. Sharing such a secret between two creates a synthetic bond. The bond is only as strong as the secrecy.

This fun and excitement is deceitful. As soon as the danger of discovery or fatality presents itself, the fun and excitement scatters. Discovery means that the significant others find out. This could ruin the lives of children. Even careers if the person is a well-known figure.

Fatality can present itself in various forms. An angry lover could hurt the cheater. There is a show called Snapped to prove my point. The fatality could disguise itself in the form of an untreatable sexually transmitted disease like AIDs or Herpes.

When I examine my own cheating and others, the reasons are hardly justifiable if the cheater's goal is a healthy relationship. I find that the reasons are birth from restlessness or misconception of relationships. A woman will cheat on a man she perceives is not paying attention to her. I say perceives because he could just be occupied with a work project.

Instead of communicating her feelings, she will use it as an excuse to frolic with her crush. I have heard men say "if she does not give it to me, I have to get it from somewhere." They take this cliché as a pass to ride the infidelity train. The whole time they fail to understand the permanent damage they are doing in the name of a temporary feeling.

Then there is this crazy phenomenon that occurs. There are women and men that should end their relationship and they do not. A man could be beating the crap out of a woman. That woman will stand by that man until common sense or death makes a better decision for her.

I would think that they one being beaten would cheat. I would think that the one being ignored for work would stay. My focus is the one that is cheating for selfish reasons. Suck it up and occupy your time with something that builds your future. If you have time to cheat, you have time to make money.

Speaking of money, this is another relationship distraction. Everyone goes into a relationship with their personal perception of money. Each person has their own money habits embedded in them through their developmental influences. Sometimes two people can meet with aligning money values. This is rare though.

The purchases a person makes is reflective of their habits and interest. Those purchases may not seem imperative to someone with differing habits and interest. Simply put, he might want to buy something. She might think it is a waste of money.

The couples in the longest relationships deal with this issue. It becomes a distraction when the issue becomes bigger than the relationship's peace. Many couples make the mistake of waiting until there is an issue to address money. This is a mistake.

When a couple realizes they are merging, especially in the area of finance, they should stop and talk. The older I get, I realize no one wants to discuss money. I think this is foolish. Why ignore something that dictates daily life?

Having positive talks about budgets and money expectations early in the relationship can reduce these distractions. When the couple has unaligned money values, they can proactively problem solve. This beats waiting until a financial set beck to reveal the lack of alignment. If the agreement stage is reached, there is no problem with personal purchases. Unless one party breaches the agreement.

Some people are spenders. Some people are savers. Some people are investors. Some people are debt hoarders. It is important to identify money perspectives as early in the relationship as possible.

Life circumstances can also distract relationships. No one commits to a relationship because they think it is doomed. The life, vitality, and potential of a partner compels us to take the serious steps in life with them. However, circumstances can distract and deceive us from what we initially sign up for.

Sickness may be my most heart tugging one. I am dealing with a friend whose husband has stage 4 cancer. For seventeen years, he took great care of his wife and family. Now, he is helpless by physical, financial, and emotional means.

The hardship of taking on the family's responsibilities is weighing on my friend. She is completely distracted from the life they used to have. She is now engulfed in what is right now. The happiness has been replaced with worry, doubt, and financial woes.

A lessor woman would cut her losses and run for the hills. The distraction and allure of a healthy man is tempting. No one anticipated he would become terminally ill. It is just a circumstantial distraction that they have to overcome.

Changes in careers can be the cause of a relationship to get distracted. When my partner and I became committed, I was simply a school teacher. Currently, I am a published author, business owner, student, and still working in education. As a behavior skills teacher, my job is more demanding than a normal teacher.

Juggling so many hats has caused me to be distracted. I neglect to cook as much. I forget to do menial chores I normally finish subconsciously. I do not have a as much time to tend to my partner as well.

I have to recalibrate periodically. I have to manage my time to include my relationship. I will not give a pass for infidelity because I am distracted. Still, it is not right for him to go daily being ignored. I am proactive by acknowledging my responsibilities in a relationship and prioritizing my time.

Another selfish relationship distraction can be old issues. Let's be clear, this is not about reoccurring issues. There is a difference between used to happen and still happening. I want to prevent others from being distracted by what used to happen or past wounds.

I must admit, it is hard to look past old situations. The past informs me of a person's future capabilities. If a person is accused of being a serial killer, I will handle him going forward as a serial killer. I will keep my distance.

This response is not plausible in a relationship. In a relationship there will be hurtful times. Even after getting past the adversity, the residual effects can still haunt a couple. This is the distraction I want to address.

Once you have caught someone red handed, you will not forget it. You can forgive them. You can stay committed to them, but you will not forget the offense. This will cause you to be distracted by looking for signs of the offense happening again.

This looking to catch instead of being surprised is justifiable. Being justified does not make it less dangerous. Harping on old issues steal time for current peace and building. You will fail to see the beauty of the now by living in the yesterday.

Your inner thoughts will eventually manifest themselves directly or indirectly. If you make up your mind to forgive someone, then do that. Forgive and live as if the offense never occurred until you have solid proof of otherwise. Spend more time together in love than apart and suspicious.

The fear of old issues is a detrimental distraction. It can lead one into a mental abyss of negative thinking. Again, no one commits to doom. When a partner breaks our trust, it makes us wonder what else they might do. That wondering is a distraction.

The worst kind of old issues are the ones from previous relationships. Poor unsuspecting partners find themselves tangled up with a new person and their old past. A woman will treat a new man like a cheater if her only interactions in relationship has been with cheaters. A man may not trust his new girlfriend if his old girlfriend cheated on him.

Instead of fighting what may come, fight for what will be. No positive outcomes will be a result of negative thinking. It is ok to trust your gut. Just do not let your gut be the reason you are unreasonable and alone.

There will always be a fear of something when you are in a relationship. Especially when you hear and see the shady things people do to their partners. If you take in too much of the negative distractions, you will naturally see it in your own relationship. Focus on the positives and promote peace in your relationship.

There are many outside distractions that will come against your union. Make sure you take care not to be that distraction yourself. So many people self-sabotage healthy relationships. Keeping control in a healthy fashion can prevent such sabotaging.

When a person takes care of the distractions mentioned above, it makes it hard for outside influences to disrupt a peaceful union. An outside distraction easily makes itself at home between a couple that is internally distracted. I doubt they will openly admit it, but there are people waiting on the downfall of good relationships. Their motives are selfish of course.

There are women and men out there that do not respect the principal of commitment. They will test the relationship of individuals they want to pursue in conceited motives. They will make lavish promises. They will make relationship breaking suggestions.

If you and your partner have solidified the goals of your finances, duties to one another, and healed from the past it will be tougher for these distractions to win your attention. Most people only want you because of your perceived value. They have no clue how crazy you are. You have no idea what they are capable of.

I am not advocating that anyone stay in a hellish relationship. Abuse is abuse. I am not advocating that anyone leave for any one reason. I do want to caution couples of relationship distractions.

I personally believe some distractions are a non-negotiable. There are some distractions I am ok with accepting. All of this is relevant to the individual and their desired relationship outcomes. Just do not let go of your future relationship for a now distraction.

Chapter 5: Mental Distractions

Mental distractions in my opinion are the most detrimental of them all. Mental distractions can be invisible to the naked eye. They are not tangible like mistresses and overspent money. Still the presence of mental distractions can be just as eroding. Maybe even more.

One can identify a relationally distracted man by his infidelity. It is easy to spot a financially distracted woman when her finances are pledged to frivolous spending habits. The spiritually distracted are marked by their lack of moral compass and respect of values. Mental distractions take a bit more digging to expose.

Some mental distractions are as harmless as sulking over a failed exam. Things happen daily that cause us to give negative energy attention. We are human. The dangerous part of giving negative energy attention is the possibility of not moving past it by a reasonable time.

Negativity only begets negativity. Sometimes we become distracted by so many small negative things, life seems like a big negative blur. You have to proactively throw off negative distractions with positive affirmations. This is easier said than done.

Let's look at the exam example. If I make a failing grade in my first class and negate to throw it off, it will amplify the negativity of the next negative occurrence. If I fail to throw off the next few negative distractions, the negativity starts to snowball. By the end of the day, I will think I had a terrible day.

The reality is, my day is not terrible, I am just letting mental distractions blind me to positive aspects of my day. The negativity also prevents me from making rational decisions about how to improve my day. Negative thoughts are like cancer. They eat away at positivity and consume your mental space with their negativity.

I like to call mental distractions phantoms. We fight them and their potential harm daily. We rarely stop to acknowledge that half of the things we were distracted by in the past never came to fruition. This truth alone should prevent one from indulging in negative mental distractions.

These phantoms haunt our goals and future dreams. They remind us of our inconsistencies and lack of resources. They prevent us from taking vital and initial steps to success. They stand in the way of those that yield to them and steal their potential for success.

These phantoms invade our present too. They constantly remind us of losing our current status. This can be at work, home, or various areas in life. They try to entice us to give up. These phantoms are not age biased.

They lie to us that others are against us. Sadly, those same people do not have us in mind. They are too busy fighting their own phantoms. Keep this in mind when someone gives you a "vibe" as you read their facial expression. Yes, they possess a vibe, just maybe not concerning you.

Everyday stressors give life to the mental distractions or phantoms. Most of us interact with others throughout our day. Some do have the luxury of staying isolated in their home three hundred and sixty-five days of the week, I think. People bring uncontrollable variables that we respectfully tolerate.

Human error brings unforeseen circumstances. Sometimes these errors are not committed by us, but they still affect us. Everyday a new challenge presents itself as a new mental distraction depending on your agenda. I work in behavior, I wrestle with negativity for a living.

Other phantoms purposely come from your past to mentally distract you. They remind you of past sins and shortcomings. They threaten you with exposing new associates to old skeletons. They will isolate you with fear of what happened to stunt what will be.

Mental distractions from your past play on failed attempts as well. When the greatest philosophers and successful people in the world are asked the key to success, they almost all agree on failure. They use failure as a strategy to extrapolate learning opportunities. They meet failure with open arms knowing failure is a component of success.

If you are average, failure can have a devastating effect on you. I think people forget everyone fails. Instead of letting it go, a mentally distracted person will facilitate negative thoughts about failure. They will use failure as an excuse to not try again.

The whole while, no one is aware you are fighting a single thing. This is what makes mental distractions so dangerous. Loved ones can intervene where they see need. Everyone is not strong enough to cry for help. Some are too ashamed to.

I have found that people that are highly and mentally distracted live very haphazard lives. As a disclaimer, I am not living to my fullest potential. I am still working to reach my personal goals and pinnacles. However, you can tell I am going somewhere.

I can tell when others are going somewhere as well. We all are susceptible to mental distractions. The ones that yield to the negative and unprofitable ones the most are obvious too. I am so sure because I used to struggle with some of the same distractions.

Self-discipline must be mastered or almost mastered to beat mental distractions. The discipline will teach you to set goals. It will give you the tools to meet the goal. Earl Nightingale said that most people cannot reach goals because the process becomes boring.

Mental distractions might be the most deceitful of all distractions. Beside the phantoms, a person has to control the illusion of their perception. When a person is highly enraged, their perception of most things will be negative. If a person is experiencing unflinching peace, they can extrapolate positivity from the worse scenario.

Even though I struggle with anger, I believe it is safer to choose peace on purpose. Peace softens the spirit and clears the mind. I think the spirit is the gateway to the mentality. Our mentality is the reaction to what our spirits receive continuously.

Therefore, if you constantly receive peace, you tend to be a peaceful person. The angered let negative energy manifest inside until it is excreted through their actions. When we let mental distractions and negative energy in, we run the risk of infecting our mental state. Medical books call this phenomenon mental illness.

I am not a doctor. Nothing in this book should be taken as medical advice. There are people with mental illnesses caused by heredity and medical factors. There is also a population of people who suffer from self-inflicted mental illness.

I have seen two things be true in my life. One, a man was given a two week's notice to live. At the time, he worked three jobs. He went to work seven days a week. This was two years ago.

He is in his 70's and alive and well. He currently picks his grandkids up from school. He was forced to retire, but he is still enjoying life. He has physical restrictions, but he prefers that over time restrictions on his life.

Two, another person in my life is constantly ill. She watches all types of shows that expose her to various diseases. She is constantly looking up every hurt and tingle to diagnose herself. When she hears of a new prognosis, she aligns herself to fit the criteria.

The first person was focused on healing. Let's be clear, yes it takes more than focus. You cannot smoke, drink, and eat junk food for 60 years and expect a miracle. Still, part of healing is focus.

The second person is still to this day complaining of some ailment. That time she is taking to be distracted by phantoms of sickness, could be used to manifest profits. She has had this habit for so many years, at this point it is a negative hypnotic rhythm. I believe this is a scary mental distraction to have.

One person is mentally focused. He refused to allow a trained medical professional steer his destiny. He had the power to think for himself. He could have chosen to accept the death sentence.

The other person is not dead. But how alive are you when you are constantly distracted by something not happening? The more she allows herself to be mentally distracted, the more time she triggers her body to manifest the sickness. You see the folly in mental distractions yet?

I grew up believing that if you heard voices in your head you were crazy. I do not believe anyone specifically told me that. I gathered that information from seeing tv and people with "voices in their head". It was assumed knowledge.

The struggle was, I heard voices in my head. I used to try and suppress it with music or directed thoughts. As I grew up, I realized those voices were not voices. It was my mentality, my thoughts.

I just attributed it to voices because it is how I naturally receive information, through sound. The mentality is the thing that reminds me to remind myself. The mentality is an accumulation of all images and sounds I have been exposed to. It gives me encouragement or discouragement depending on my choice.

The mentality is not biased. It is not a tyrant. It allows us to indulge in the energy of our choosing. If we allow mental distractions in, it receives them with open arms. If we decide to ignore mental distractions, it rolls with that decision to.

A person has to be a steward over their mentality. Mental distractions can come wrapped in pretty bows. Mental distractions will present themselves in the form of a handsome man. Mental distractions can be something you in fact enjoy.

I suffer from mental distractions. I do not know who does not. The important thing is managing those distractions. This is where goals play another role.

If you formulate goals and timelines, you are less likely to be mentally distracted. If you lack self-discipline this will not work. The goals serve as a time filler. Goals just happen to also have the benefit of building futures too. Positive goals that is.

Mental distractions do not always have an evil agenda. Sometimes we have to mentally distract ourselves to save ourselves. I get it. I just advise one never to stay mentally distracted too long.

Always recalibrate and bring yourself back to reality. Being mentally distracted on purpose is a sign you are running from something. At some point you have to stop running and start winning. Winning is found in finishing.

Mental distractions hinder a person from finishing. They induce stagnancy and failure. They may even feel good. The reality is, there is a reality. Being focused is the only way to positively change any reality.

Chapter 6: Social Distractions

Social distractions are a double-edged sword for me. Social distractions have to happen to sustain life. Too many social distractions make life stagnant. Social distractions present themselves everywhere we go.

Social distractions are at work. Most people have that one coworker they gravitate to. After being at a company or organization for a while, some people form homogenous groups. It is not on purpose. It is a natural occurrence.

We are naturally inclined to be around people like us. Think about your best friend. You guys have similarities that motivate you two to be around each other. You have the same propensities and habits that cause you to spend time together.

We are naturally repelled from those that have differing opinions and propensities. If our dislikes move us to the emotion of hatred or anger, it becomes prejudice. We tend to avoid people we do not prefer, even at work. I am super guilty of taking another route if I see someone I do not prefer to be socially distracted by.

Social distractions at work prevent optimum productivity. This is why budgets make room for supervisors and bosses. They are responsible for seeing that employees are focused on work. Bosses are the social distraction police at work.

The thing is they fail. We still find a way to talk to our work buddies about something other than work. We still find a way to do task at work that have nothing to do with work. The best companies and organizations know how to appropriately manage this issue with systems and policies.

Social distractions interrupt your goals in various forms. My biggest Achilles heel is social events. When I was in high school, it seemed easier to make events with friends. Now it seems almost impossible.

The problem has been I am always working or in school. These hobbies give me obligations that require effort at social hours. Having a full-time job and completing degrees makes a Birthday party a social distraction. I had to trade my party life for a life of books and responsibilities.

Friends and family members can receive the wrong perception if they have differing values. Some are big enough to recognize the difference and have a mutual respect. Most will not. They will receive your absence as a lack of loyalty or envy.

When your goals are bigger than people's perception, it is easier to avoid social distractions. The opinion and perception of others drive many to be socially distracted instead. That is the deceit. You can be caught in the distraction of a loved one's event or caught in building your future.

The digital age makes being socially distracted seem routine. Thanks to social media, people are socially distracted today more than ever. Before the cell phone and digital apps, social distractions had to be sought after. Now, apps and device notifications let a person know every time a new social distraction is available.

I have no issue with social media. I believe it is a necessary and powerful tool. My problem is with the socially distracted people on social media. The ones that use the medium for distraction purposes only.

Social media does not have much biased. The people that interact on social media possess all the biases. However, the program software itself is pretty welcoming to whomever. Some do have age restrictions.

You can have a social media account if you are rich or poor. The account process will not lock you out due to ethnicity prejudiced. If you have the technology to access the internet, you can create a social media profile. You may need to be able to read a little bit. But literacy is not a prerequisite.

On all social media outlets I am a part of, there are people who clearly have their priorities out of place. You see people with children posting things that their kids are later ridiculed about. There are others that are in desperate need of better living wages to elevate their standard of living. Others are spending their time reposting the glorified garbage.

This may be the biggest form of social distraction to me. Those mentioned above will give you a million reasons for their current conditions. They will blame everyone in their past that refused to give them a handout. They will do everything but identify their faults. They are light years away from changing their destructive habits.

They fail to realize they possess all they need to be successful. They will remain in their social distractions until they have a burning desire for better. Everyone wants better. Few are willing to give up their social distractions for it.

The irony is the same participation that social media requires, is the same participation schools and training programs require. The same people that claim college is hard, are actually doing college like assignments on social media daily. The very same person that claim they have no time, probably spend more time on social media than college requires. The effort requirement matches as well.

The same social distraction that social media produces is a social interaction in college or training. A person receives communication via social media. This communication can be a real person. Sometimes the communication is a post that requires reading.

Social media participants are distracted by people and events from all over the world. People have the ability to hold causal conversations with others from another country. They interact digitally and form relationships as if in person. More global interactions mean more knowledge is dispersed and faster.

Unless they have blocked everyone, composed post are available to the world. Even the ones in seemingly private pages. Once received the other social media participants respond. The poster has the ability to analyze, respond, or ignore.

In the same manner a person receives communication via their college course. The communication can be initiated by the professor or a colleague. It may be in video form or written. Just as on social media.

In college, interacting with a diverse population is second nature. Colleges and universities bring people together from various backgrounds and cultures. Talking with inhabitants of other regions and locations gives the college student a wider perspective in life. Meeting new people brings new information. Just like on social media.

The college student then analyzes and responds to the above-mentioned communication. They take in external factors and varying perspectives. They formulate an educated response or not. Just like in social media.

When you look at some people's social media, they have been a member since the early 2000s. Here we are going into 2020. Those people that have posted to social media for close to a decade or more could all have degrees by now. Instead they have spent numerous years being socially distracted.

College Required Post:

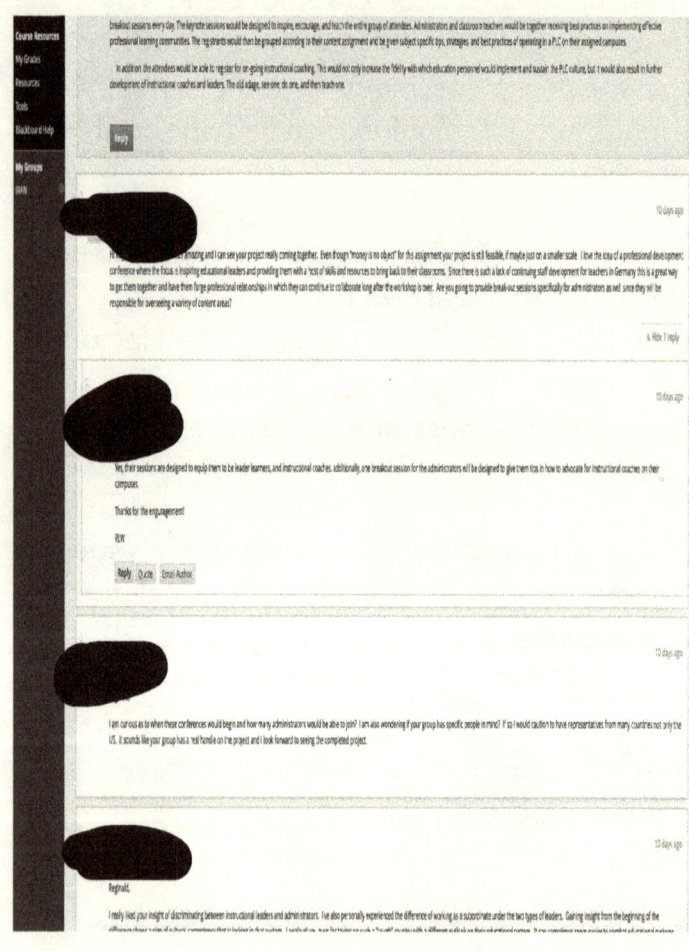

Social Media Post:

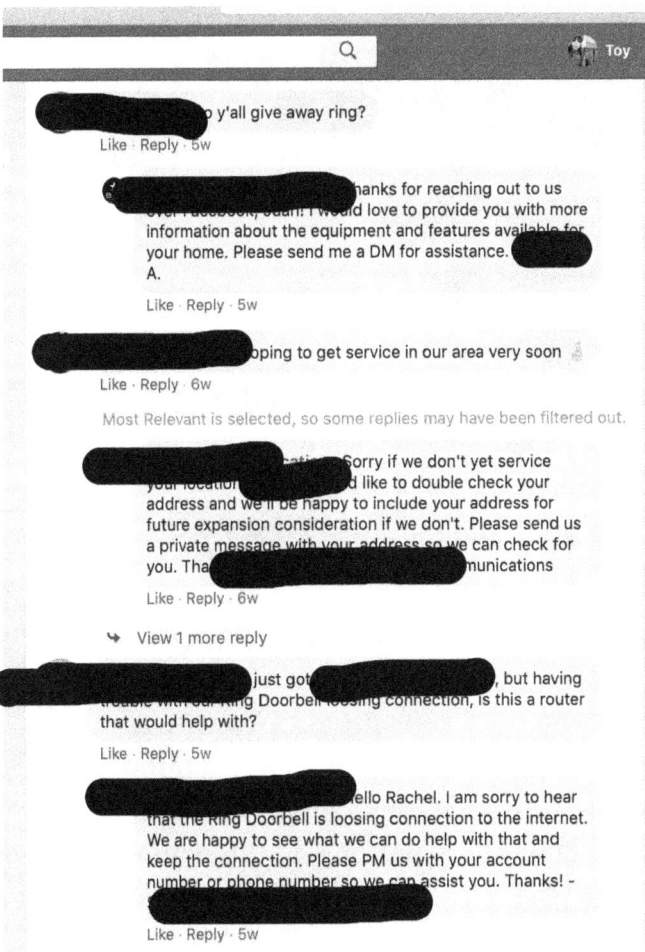

😥😥😥
💥🔥💥🔥

███ i just got word that a scream queens reboot is reportedly in the works! if so, please please 🙏 retake your role as ███ 😍 she is a fun cop 🤍 love you!!!

███ May your birth month be filled with tears of joy, hugs of laughter, and screams of adventures!! You are a true treasure to so many, thank you for sharing bits and pieces of your life with us. GOD BLESS you richly in the name of JESUS

Notice the social media post had more engagement then the college post?

This same scenario is true of all social distractions. That time that is used to soak up the lives and moves of others is valuable. The perceived value is sometimes enough to get people started. It takes continuous focus to stay the course.

You have to manage your social distractions just like the distractions. Failing to take control of social distractions will lead to a life of watching, but never doing. This is only ok if you have no goals or ambition. To each his own.

Chapter 7: Manufactured Distractions

Some distractions are self-imposed. Some distractions are welcomed. Some distractions naturally occur with life and time. Some distractions are straight up manufactured.

Distractions equate to power and profit when used for such gains. I do not want to give these distractions a sinister connotation. I do want you to be aware that someone or organization is trying to distract you on purpose. The most lucrative big business is obviously succeeding.

Thanks to the technological advancements in the Information Age, big gains are to be paid to the biggest distractions. The gain can be profitable for both the business and the consumer. It just depends on what that distraction is. We live in a world that pays top dollar to whoever creates the biggest distraction.

This only poses a problem for the consumer who buys unprofitable distractions. It is possible to be distracted all the time and have wealth as a result. Some of the biggest innovators and wealthiest people alive today prove this theory. It seems that Bill Gates was distracted with his business idea when he dropped out of Harvard.

This leads me to the original definition of distraction. Earlier in the selection, I wanted to focus only on negative distractions. I wanted to be clear about the distractions that support our stagnancy. Going back to Webster's original definition, it takes a profitable distraction to eradicate an unprofitable distraction.

You are either distracting others or being distracted yourself. Which one are you? The biggest distractors get paid the biggest amounts. Instead of being caught staring at the distractions I mentioned in earlier chapters, it may do you some good to become a distraction.

Clergy, preachers, and other religious leaders profit from spiritually distracting others. People pay them sizable amounts depending on the leader's influence and following size. They assist their followers in managing their spiritual distractions. They are supposed to lead a life that is an example of their spirituality.

Religious leaders specialize in their craft like doctors. They are supposed to commit themselves to their perspective discipline or religion. They study and become familiar with the details of their specified religion. When they have been ordained or deemed ready, they relay their revelations of their teachings to others.

Some religious leaders do have jobs separate from their ministry income. Many that I know depend solely on their ministry to provide a living for themselves. I do not think this is wrong. I just want to point out how and why spiritual distractions are manufactured.

It is your job to personally decide which spiritual distraction you take heed to. Make sure you are giving more attention to the spiritual distractions that builds your spirit instead of tear it down. Be mindful that some distractions will present themselves as supporters of your spirituality. In actuality they are working for the other side. Stay aware.

I revealed earlier that some are wealthy because of their financial distractions. I also made it clear that some are poor because of financial distractions. It is the wealthy often time distracting the poor. Which side of the distraction do you fall on again?

Unless they are living on old money, wealthy people become a distraction because they see the potential profit. They have identified the folly in spending in unprofitable distractions. They may still have unprofitable habits. The trick is making sure the profitable ones have priority majority of the time.

Without malice, people build businesses. Some invent products to help others or serve a need. Others create an idea that creates paradigm shifts in industries. The common goal is to manufacture a distraction that produces financial profits.

They then use those profits to pay for their own unprofitable distraction. The poor man works and trades their own time for manufactured distractions. The poor have the same opportunity as the wealthy to become a distraction. Sadly, their negative hypnotic rhythms keep them bound to being distracted.

The manufacturing of distractions for relationships is a bit more complicated. There are two ways that I want to focus on. One you have to watch out for more vigilantly than the other. I will start with the less complicated way.

Big businesses profit from romance just like everything else. They will use the sanctity of love to make the almighty dollar if they have to. If you look at all love takes according to society, they do this rightly so. This is a case where both parties benefit from manufactured distractions.

If you think about a wedding alone, can you see the opportunity for a manufactured distraction. Can you understand how a distraction can lead to a profit? The big business has no malicious intent, I think. It is just, if you are going to buy a dress, they want to sell it to you.

Selling it means creating a distraction. Manufacturing a campaign that will entice brides is a part of the distraction. A dress is just one component. If you think of everything that goes into an average wedding, there is much room for manufactured distraction.

The other way a relationship can be affected by a manufactured distraction is unwarranted attention. In the chapter that covered relationship distractions, I focused on the two that were in the relationship. I talked about the distractions that they typically partake in. Sometimes couples are disturbed by manufactured distractions instead of personal ones, in a negative way.

There is a certain type of woman and man that exists that respects no moral boundaries. They are not deterred by the fact that someone they are interested in has a significant other. They will make advances and attempts to ruin a happy home. All for the allure of their own selfish desires.

They will bug a person's mate even when there is no response. They are so distracted themselves by the fantasy in their head, they make advances past open rejection. They hang on to the deceitful promises of persistence. They hope their being adamant will pay off.

This is the worst kind of manufactured distractions for a couple. Sick people will tell believable lies hoping to break a family down. They attack relationship foundations by making sure the couple is distracted from their happiness. If a couple is not careful and secure, they will fall prey.

Mental distractions, like spiritual distractions, have "appointed" leaders as well. They are usually self-made or accomplished people that have faced great adversity. They use their stories and strategies as a way to motivate others. They manufacture distractions in various mediums to address their followers.

They write books. They host events. They make appearances as guest. They are called to inspire others to reach their highest potential.

They manufacture distractions that feed the mind and build the spirit. Their purpose is closely related to that of spiritual leaders. The big difference with mental distraction is it is intrinsic. Positive mental distractions require the distracted to pull from within.

Spiritual distractions are aligned to a higher purpose or power. They cause one to depend on an intangible entity through faith. Mental distractions keep the focus on the person searching for the distraction. They put the work of being positive on the person.

Social distractions that are manufactured normally have a focused purpose. Since socializing with people brings profits, socializing is a way of life for some. Social media, institutional attendance, and other networking events can be manufactured as well. The difference between my current reference and my past one is motive.

It is one thing to attend a social engagement to "get away" or "strut". It is another to attend that same social engagement to network and build contacts. I would say both participants are distracted by the social engagement. But one is being socially distracted with a purpose.

I have the same sentiments towards social media. It is not the medium that distracts. It is the user and their motivation for logging in. Social media has proven to be a lucrative marketing tool. Even for myself.

When I actively advertise on social media, I see sales and customer engagement. When I do not, I see lesser results. So, I can attest to the value in having a social media profile. It opens up a global gateway and makes commerce available to the common.

Businesses use profiles to promote and prospect for new customers. Did I mention it was free? In a world that pays top dollar for marketing, social media is free. It is profitable when you spend more time socially distracting than being distracted.

Manufactured distractions, like all distractions can have a good or bad connotation. The interpretation is always related to the motives and morals of a person. They are a medium. They can help us stay connected with the positive. They can also help us stay connected with the negative, if that is what we choose to do.

It takes honesty to identify manufactured distractions and their role in your life. It takes courage to reroute amongst others when you realize you are distracted. Self-discipline will be your best friend in remaining free of that manufactured distraction that brings you no profit.

I recommend sorting through manufactured distractions you perceive have profit. All distractions cost you time. A resource that is unrecoverable. Rank these types of distractions.

Give priority to the ones that have the most perceived value. Failing to do so could cause an individual to waste time on task of lesser value. You want to get the most value for the time you spend right? You want to live your best life, right?

As you sort the manufactured distractions, you will get to comb through how you spend time. When you rank them, you will be exposed to the true value of your expended time. After you prioritize the law of attraction should bring what you want.

Manufactured distractions are not the solution to unprofitable and selfish distractions. They are tools to support the productive use of your time. They are instrumental in keeping commerce fluid. They play whatever role the user chooses for them to play.

I warn you that you carefully search the origins of manufactured distractions. What glitters is not always gold indeed. I believe I have said this already, but some distractions wrap themselves up in a pretty bow. They bite the hand of those who reach out to touch it.

The most profitable manufactured distractions will cost. Besides time, they may require intellectual effort. They may be harder to obtain than less profitable ones. This makes discernment an ally when making those choices.

Chapter 8: The Deceit

I am positive that I missed some other distractions that people struggle with. My intention was to explain a limited range to paint a picture of various distractions. I then wanted the reader to interpret there are distractions to be found in multiple areas of their lives. Finally, I set out to complete the definition of distractions.

When I completed the definition, my goal was to express all distractions are not bad distractions. I do not want the reader to walk away hating distractions. It is more important that they manage them. Most cannot afford living in a dark soundproof attic that shields them from distractions.

Even there, one is left with the distraction of their own thoughts. Identifying and managing distractions is imperative to dodging it's deceit. I mentioned earlier that one should identify the origins of distractions. This will also make one privy to it's deceit.

Everyone has fallen victim to the deceit of distractions. Sometimes voluntarily. Sometimes involuntarily. The important thing to do is recognize when we are being distracted. Then either choose to avoid it or make it profitable.

When we fall into the deceit of distractions on purpose, there is not much to say. Sometimes we know that we are being distracted and we enjoy it. For example, I love to play video games. So much I was willing to fail school remember?

This voluntary distraction brings me no perceived profit. It is strictly for recreational use. It makes me feel relaxed and relieved. The relaxation and relief are both part of the deceit.

The release of endorphins makes me happy for the present time. The time I take to immediately gratify myself could be used for future building. The relaxation and relief in a sense are holding me back. This is just a micro example.

Imagine the magnitude of deceit the distraction of heroin delivers to it's users. This drug, and others, will compel mothers to leave their children. I saw a woman in the news recently who sold her kids sexually for drugs. Anything that makes a mother believe they should sell their child for anything, is deceit. That person is bound by the ultimate distractions.

I kept my vantage point on the lessor distractions for a reason. Some, like a crack addict, are obvious. Yet, some are stealthy. They seem harmless. You do not grip the full extent of their damage until it is done.

Spiritual distraction are the ones I try to avoid most. I will not get in-depth about my religious views. I will say they are strong enough to keep me from following some entities and organizations. Being spiritually distracted for me is like playing Russian Roulette with my soul.

This is not to say I am perfect. I fall short. I am working to be better. However, there are some lines I do not cross. I understand crossing them opens me up to forces I want no parts of.

Still some do. I watch. Many become unaware of their mortality. This happens over time for several reasons. The individual may achieve momentous success. They could possibly do negative deeds without detection well. The list goes on.

This type of person fails to heed the spiritual and scientific laws that warn them. This is the deceit at work. Even if they are taught right from wrong, their perception will be distorted based on exposure and experiences. If a bank robber successfully robs four or five banks, they are likely to make a career out of it. The one that is caught the first time is more inclined to stop.

The national debt in America is the best symbol of financial distraction I have ever seen. I also struggle with financial distractions myself. The glittering things of today are so enticing. They are so enticing that some are willing to throw away their tomorrow away for it.

The saddest thing to me is, I do not have to even possess the money to throw my tomorrow away. Credit companies give me lines of credit to fund my distractions. Payday loan companies demand my financial keys and codes for quick gratification. These places fund social, mental, relationship, heck all the distractions.

Those same financial institutions could be used for investment loans. They could put our kids through college. Instead our kids are graduating with debt that equates to a mortgage. All the while they have nowhere to stay. All for the deceit of our distractions.

I am guilty. I am pointing no fingers. I had to do some major credit repair once I graduated college. Once I realized I was distracted. Once I focused in on my end.

Seeing people I love go into retirement made me focus up. They hailed retirement while I was in school. They made it seem like a endless honeymoon. And it can be. If you retire a certain way.

They people I am watching retire are not doing so well. For my level of comfortability. They are having to pinch and scrape because they retired with too much debt. They have no cash flowing income.

Their set retirement check is no match for the inflation of the dollar.

    They find themselves having to go back to work. It is often right back where they retired from. They do not possess the will power to learn new skills. They do not have the vitality and charisma to beat a younger person out of the job.

    This is not true of all retirees. It is true of the financially distracted retirees. I was a financially distracted child. I was a financially distracted teenager. I was a financially distracted young adult.

    I am trying to change my dynamic. It was painful at first, but the rewards eventually manifest themselves. The biggest pain was psychological. Once I got over what opinions might be given, the rest was fairly workable.

    The fear of being homeless is more important to me than anyone's opinion. I cannot depend on the government. I am not above it, life happens. I do not want to. With the political climate we have, depending on them is like depending an absent baby daddy.

    What is one to do if the well runs dry? What if the well is poisoned? What if it is shut off? It is 2019, we have already had a government shutdown. Families were struggling because of it. Good families.

    You are either a worker ant, or a leech. Which is It? I hope it is a worker ant. Leeches are burned off and forgotten.

Chapter 9: The Choice

You have to purposely choose to not be distracted. It is a skill that has to be developed. There is more to it than just telling yourself "I will not be distracted". Becoming your most productive self and your least distracted self is a process.

I have not met anyone that revealed a secret way to do this yet. It takes time and process monitoring. The idea to be our most productive selves is conceived almost instantaneously. The time of conception distracts us from the reality of making the idea tangible.

Good ideas make us feel happy at first. Once the reality begins to set in, the distractors are separated from the distracted. A distractor will stay focused on bringing the idea to fruition. They may even get distracted along the way.

Their being distracted does not last for long. They eventually recalibrate and focus on the idea. Self-disciplined people practice this on a regular basis. This is why they are able to make their ideas tangible.

They do not have super powers. They do not possess a magic pill that makes them limitless. They may possess some pills. Just not magic ones.

They are simply not hindered by their distractions. This is the opposite of the distracted person. When they are met with the reality of making ideas tangible, their response is polar opposite. This is why their success is not as measurable as the most successful.

Some of the distracted are excited enough to initiate the process. Some are not. They are held back by lack of resources. They let the fear of ostracism keep them frozen in place.

The distracted that are bold enough to start meet the initial requirements, only keep their steam for a while. As they go along with the process to bring their idea to fruition, they initially get distracted. They get distracted by the distractions I listed previously in this literature. They can also become distracted by the distractions I left out on purpose.

They become bored with the process. Eventually, the glimmer of the idea is dimmed by the reality of the work it takes. The excitement of the future is outweighed by the immediate gratification of the present. They do not leave the idea with the intention of abandonment.

They leave with the intention of returning after indulging in their distraction. The distraction eventually takes hold of them. Before they know it, they have left the idea. They will pick up the next grand idea and repeat this fruitless cycle.

The deceit is in the distraction seeming harmless. It is not until the person passes their due date, they realize the deceit of their distraction. It is at this point the distracted person is presented with an opportunity. Every time a person fails at a goal, they have an opportunity.

They have the opportunity to continue to be distracted. They can be distracted even more by the threat of failing regardless of restarting. Or they can take another approach. Again, it will not be easy.

They can realize what distracted them and manage that distraction. A good example of this is a college dropout that returns to school. The time line of which they return varies. Some people take a semester off. Some people take a couple of years.

The most important thing is they realize the value of their education above their distraction. This brings them the same degree that the less distracted obtain. The degree does not reveal how long it took to obtain. I admire these people.

The magnitude of management that a distraction takes depends on the distraction. A more complicated distraction will take more effort to manage. A less complicated distraction will take less effort to manage. It also depends on the circumstance of the individual. Consider this truth when ranking distractions.

Sometimes when my high school athletes get new significant others, they become distracted. I can tell by their performance in school and on the court. They are more concerned with the new beaux than their own success. The process of managing this distraction is not so complicated normally.

As the coach, I see the students during more of their waking hours than the parents. I first try talking with the athlete. If that fails, I then involve the parents. We normally are able to put the child back on track. There has been one extreme case that became complicated.

A new significant other can be a very complicated distractions if the circumstances change. Let's say a married man acquires a new significant other. This will take more managing than a phone call to his parents. He hypothetically has a whole wife and family to answer to.

The wife will notice that the husband is distracted just as I notice my athletes are. If she has no hard evidence, she will become distracted by watching his comings and goings. All the while, time is being stolen from them both.

If she finds the evidence of what she is looking for, she will now have a whole new distraction. She and the husband will have to problem solve. Taking more time. They are not in high school.

If they decide to remain married, they will have the complications of managing his fidelity. If they make the decision to divorce, they then have the complication of severing the relationship. Dissolving a marriage can take years under rough circumstances. Same distraction. Different magnitude of management because of the circumstances.

There are some common ways to break distractions that are not so complicated. They are universal techniques. When used appropriately they can help us stay focused on our goals instead of being distracted. The more focus we have, the less likely we are to be distracted.

One way is to track your time. It might be the simplest way. Tracking your time will help you pinpoint real time you have to be productive. This is as simple as writing out an profitable daily task on a pad.

Then evaluate each daily task. Check it's potential for profits and make it a priority accordingly as I mentioned in previous chapters. After this is done, you now have the tools to make a plausible schedule. If you make a schedule without consideration of certain factors, it will be hard to keep that schedule.

My favorite tool for preventing distractions is scheduling. Not just any scheduling. Scheduling for my goals. I am not too fond of other schedules.

The scheduling that mandates me to make someone else's goal come to fruition is less appealing. You have to be mindful of this. You have to guard your own schedule. There is a benefit of being distracted and available to others.

Like other distractions, this has to be managed. You will be able to see the time you commit to other's goals when you miss the time constraints of your own schedule. If you do not schedule, you run the risk of fulfilling everyone else's dreams. The problem with that is, yours are never reached.

Scheduling not only saves me from others, it saves me from myself. If I get off my schedule it shows by my lack of productivity. Procrastination seeps in easily if I am not mindful of what I mandated myself to do. Without a schedule it is easy for me to get caught up in the day's decisions.

I also use deadlines for myself a lot. Deadlines and schedules are very similar. They both utilize time as a guiding factor. They both announce expiration of time to reach the desired result.

Deadlines differ from schedules in a few ways though. Firstly, a deadline gives you a date. That date is different from the orchestration of task that a schedule takes. A deadline focuses on a project as a whole. A schedule focuses on the individual task that need to be completed before the deadline.

An individual can also establish a distraction free area for themselves. This place should be designated only for productivity. Your family members and those close to you should know about this designated area. When you are here it should signal a few things.

It should signal to your family that you should only be disturbed for emergencies. It is best to establish this boundary early on. The kids and the significant others invade the space if not. When they invade the space, the individual becomes distracted.

Noise in the designated area is up to the individual. Sometimes I personally prefer noise. Sometimes I do not. I have two designated areas.

At my designated place when my family is not home, I like natural noises. I open all the windows in the part of the house I am in. I like to hear the sounds of the winds, the birds, even the lawn mowers. I like the melody of my neighborhood, I guess.

Ironically, when my family is home, I need a quieter space. They disrupt the peace of the neighborhood sounds. Those sounds are trampled by the life they bring into the home. When my child is excited, I am distracted by seeing what excites her. When she is upset, I am distracted by seeing what has upset her.

It is the same scenario with her dad. Just less frequent distractions. I love them so much, I think this makes them involuntary distractions. I have to find a quiet isolated place if I want to be productive when they are around.

Recalibration is another big tool for me. Recalibration can take on many connotations like the word distraction. The type of recalibration is relevant to each individual. How they recalibrate should align to their goals.

I recalibrate by reviewing goals periodically. By periodically, I mean daily.

Sometimes that recalibration is focused on daily goals. Sometimes I have to recalibrate and make sure I am still painting my bigger picture.

Recalibration is not all about refreshing. Sometimes it is a pruning process. Some goals become obsolete with time. Failing to reach a goal does not always mean being distracted.

New ambitions may take the place of old dreams. Recalibration will reveal old task that are taking away from the new ambitions. It begins to dabble on the line of being distracted if a person fails to achieve any goals.

Some people spend much time starting many things. They also fail to finish anything. This person disguises their distracted state as being "busy". Some of them actually believe they are busy.

Do not choose being distracted all the time. Be productive more than you are distracted. Or at least make sure your distraction is profitable. Choose your goals and choose the stability of your future self.

Chapter 10: A Continuum

I have some bad news for you my faithful reader. You will not be miraculously cured from distractions because you are reading this book. The distractions will not just disappear because you have educated yourself on their stealthy ways. In fact, the distractions might amplify themselves.

Not because there are more of them. They will be amplified because you now have a keener sense of them. You can identify them more easily. Their deceit, you are aware of.

Like all knowledge, it is what you do with it. Being more aware does not make a person better. Having more knowledge does not make a person better. It is the effort they expend to make changes with that knowledge that makes them better.

Some individuals fail to reach their fullest potential because of this truth. You can have all the knowledge in the world, is has no value if it is not put into practice. It is like a poor person receiving or inheriting a large sum of money. They have the medium, but it makes them no better because they retain old habits that made them poor in the first place.

Please, do not be this person. Even if you were just reading for entertainment, I challenge you to put more effort into profits instead of distractions. I agree, money is not everything. God is (to me).

But even the humblest person would agree, money is a necessity. Unless you are content to live under a bridge. I am not. So, I "needs" that money.

Others chose the under the bridge life. I see them every day. I have much respect for them. Some of them have more intelligence than me. Some of them are out there because of distractions. Others are out there because of other perilous circumstances.

Managing and avoiding distractions is an ongoing process. The most successful people recognize and adhere to the process. The distracted stay bound by their distractions. They will even acknowledge the thing is a distraction and stay there willingly.

To be completely honest, procrastination feels good. Being lazy is a treat. I try to cut the amount of effort that I expend when I can. But the procrastination comes with a price. My laziness always catches up with me.

Time has taught me it is easier to do it now than suffer later. My environment and upbringing had taught me to do the exact opposite. Living in a world that pays top dollar for convenience, I was fooled. I had to reprogram myself and understand the real value of processes.

Every time a new distraction presents itself, I treat myself like a child. I really ask myself "what are you doing? Is it profitable or productive?". I may be deemed crazy, but I am not under a bridge.

I ask myself "does this build my future or hinder it?" These questions are painful when the distraction is something you really want. A weak-minded person will go along with the distraction. They will tell themselves "it's ok, I will be productive tomorrow". This is the deceit of distractions.

Tomorrow will come, but another distraction will present itself. As the daily distractions steal precious time, that person's goal deadlines will come and go. I am like this about my diet. Always going to start, but never on a diet.

I am well aware of the long-term effects of eating unhealthy foods. BUT I LOVE THEM! I lie to myself every day that my current hamburger will be my last for a while. I tell myself that I can go without fries.

What do I really do? I go get a hamburger the following day. I request extra salt for my fries. I even upgrade my meal if I am feeling good about myself.

I am very distracted when it comes to my diet. There is a significant population of people that are distracted when it comes to life. Enticing distractions deceive them into believing there will always be enough time. Distractions market themselves as harmless time passers.

I talk to so many older people that say "if they could do it all over again". They have taught me the folly of giving up precious time now and paying for it later. This is not to downplay who they are. I just take their wisdom and use it to my advantage.

My biggest motivation to watch my distractions is a great uncle of mine. He served in the U. S. Army during World War II and Vietnam. He was a very young man when he entered the service. He spent most of his life serving his country.

Now in his old age, he has to beg the very same government he fought to protect. He was distracted by all of the benefits of working for the government. He was promised retirement pensions and benefits. Which he receives, they just did not divulge the hell he would have to go through to receive it.

I fault both parties in the equation. However, I ultimately fault my uncle for being so distracted he did not adequately consider his future. It is not that the government hates him. It is just he is looking for assistance from and institution that needs assistance itself.

There are others that join the army for the very same reasons he did. However, their outcome is much different. I know one army vet that took his earning and started a business. By doing this, he increased his income while maintaining a steady one.

Instead of fighting with the governments about his necessities, he can pull from the extra stream of income he created. When the government finishes processing his request, after he needs it, he takes their assistance as residual gains. This man did not live haphazardly distracted by institutional promises. He laid himself a foundation to be secure with or without the governments help.

I do not have anything against government assistance. Especially for those that worked to establish the assistance and need it. I just do not want to be dependent on it. If I have to, I just have to. I do not want to.

This is the approach I take to my own career now. I too was distracted by the allure of retirement accounts and minimal health benefits. As I mentioned earlier, the people retiring around me are not having fun with that. They fear inflation more than they fear death.

I made a conscious decision to put my future first. Yes, it feels good when I spend on luxury items. The attention from strutting is intoxicating. People are addicted to it.

To me, being financially unstable and unable to work, outweighs that intoxication for me. I hold myself accountable for accomplishing goals that will make my life easier in the long run. I have also grown to a point where I am being productive for my generations. My biggest fear is my kids living in poverty.

I work to secure their futures. Still, this is not enough. I have to also actively engage in helping them manage distractions while they are young. Hopefully this will translate to their adulthood. One wrong distraction could bound them to hell. No matter how much I work or pray.

As I close, I do want to challenge you to start identifying your distractions now. The sooner the better. Being proactive is more profitable than playing blind. Hold yourself accountable.

You might be surprised. You might be expending free time on something that has the potential to bring you profit. Like the video games I play. There are video game testers and designers that get paid way more than me. However, video gaming is not my passion. Just my chosen distraction.

After identification, it is decision time. You have to decide if you will remain distracted. You have to decide if you will manage and avoid those distractions. The choice as always is yours.

I want to warn you again, time is irreplaceable. You will reach your old age. What type of life do you envision for yourself? What are you doing about that now?

Some of us have already wasted sufficient time. We cannot get it back. We can work overtime to make up for our distracted time though. Do not be distracted by the lies of being "too behind".

There was an actress that was in the most popular African America film of 2018. She did not start acting until she was good and past her 50s. Most agents will tell you, you should have started younger. She is proof positive that it is never to late to achieve your goals.

The right distraction will propel you forward. The wrong and selfish distractions hold you back. They hinder your experiences. They come to steal your most precious asset; time.

Break away from people that require you to be loyal to distractions. I did not say throw away. I said break away. If you throw them away, you may severe a potentially profitable relationship.

Breaking away will have less of an effect. If it is done properly. You have to communicate appropriately. Not even divulge all of your secrets.

You can just be honest that you need time to accomplish your goals. People that love you and want the best for you will have no problem with this. They will support you.

A lesser person may respond in negative manner. Pay that no mind. That too, is a deceitful distraction. Accept positive vibes only.

I bid you well in your quest to managing and avoiding distractions. I want it for you so you can truly live your best life. Not just dream about it. It is possible when the right components are added together.

If you fail on your first try, so what? Keep going. Keep letting go of unprofitable and selfish distractions as a practice. Eventually it will become a habit.

Thank You

-Toy

Something You can be Distracted by

A snippet from Builder's Code…

Ones desired environment can be in a variety of settings that is relative to each individual. An entrepreneur can desire to build a prestigious business. A teacher can desire to build a better classroom environment. An inner ring inhabitant can desire to build an environment for themselves and their subsequent generation.

Everyone wants to eat their fill of the finest cuisines and fart strawberries. Humans naturally and instinctively desire more and better. Most use their imaginations to visualize opportunities they would like to have or goals they would like to achieve. But applied effort towards these goals vary from person to person. It is also relative to resources and circumstances that were explained before.

A small majority do actualize their goals and see them to realization. A mass majority make mild to moderate attempts, but fail short with notable progress. Getting comfortable, changes in goals, and new circumstance are examples of reasons people fail to build in a particular area. A quarter of the population settles for little to no goal attainment with unearned help from institutions. Rich or poor; all people dream.

    With proper time management, commitment, and networking any inhabitant can build their desired environment no matter their current circumstance. There has to be a certain willingness to do in order to see goals actualize. There are some that take short cuts and shake sketchy hands to make their goals come to fruition. Some get lucky and walk away unscathed, and some are caught, exposed, and setback by a path to redemption.

    A famous coach made the comment "if you aren't cheating you aren't trying." (Smith 2015)[1] He sounds like one of the confident ones that has found success by operating outside of the laws of the universe. But what really solidifies this success? One would be

---

[1] Smith M. (2015) Joe Montana: If you ain't cheating, you ain't trying, so the Patriots are trying hard. Retrieved from https://profootballtalk.nbcsports.com/2015/10/16/joe-montana-if-you-aint-cheating-you-aint-trying-so-the-patriots-are-trying-hard/

surprised how many people triumph publicly and suffer privately.

    The universe always returns to one what they give to it. Because of this, it is not really safe to say anyone gets away with anything. It's best to take an approach of integrity when build towards the desired environment and be realistic about the requirements. That way if calamity does strike, one can focus on finding the lesson in the setback rather than fondling through guilty thoughts of phantoms that may have come back. Plant over here and reap over there; good or bad.

    When the conscious is clear one also has more free time to evaluate opportunities from a pure perspective and be creative. The visualization may pose to be the easiest part of the process when attaining the desired environment, however there is a significant number of the population who are so inflicted with ill thoughts that they fail to build anything significant. Asylums and Ghettos are proof of this.

    A person building their desired environment has to guard themselves against the aforementioned people. What is in a person will manifest itself at some point in time no matter who they are if they are not being genuine. When a builder detects a toxic person, they have to disassociate themselves as soon as possible. Protecting one's environment should take precedent over toxic gains and relationships.

  There are ways to appropriately make quick shifts, like making the appropriate associations and sharpening skills mentioned earlier. But while watching for opportunities one should also watch for indications of people that already are residents at a desired environment similar to the one they are building. There are some fellow builders that are on their way that can provide information in elevation. But if a person has a reputation of being dishonest or unpleasant, they can find themselves alienated from these opportunities.

  The builders that are on their way are the most dangerous if not handled properly. Depending on their stage, they many not openly display their desired location by present attire, they may be flat out disguised.

If a person makes the mistake of mistreating or disregarding them because of their present circumstance it could come back to haunt them in future endeavors. To safe guard themselves from this, it is important for anyone building, or not, to treat everyone with kindness and respect at all times.

    Any desired environment is reserved for anyone who is willing to engage in the process that it takes to finish to the end. The easiest way for a person to do this is to be realistic about their visualization according to their effort. Even if the goal is humongous, a builder can use strategies like building in phases. The priority should be to finish; not the speed at which it is finished. Quality has to take precedent over quantity.

    One cannot let the lack of resources stop their progress to building their desired environment. There is an important lesson to be learned in creating ways to acquire necessary resources. Beneficial relationships can be built by this practice as well. There are very wealthy parents that even practice making their offspring graze for their own food. On one of the Christly episodes, the middle son and a friend asked Mr. Christly for investment money. Instead of just handing it over, because investing seems cool right, he demanded a minimum of standards before.

The highest achieving builders have understood and moved past the notion that someone owes them. They respect the philosophy of process and operate in the mindset that they are entitled to nothing. Some start high, and some start low. Regardless of the starting location everyone has the ability to build to their desired location if they are willing to pay the price, adhere to unwritten code, and finish building.

Finally.

Education is the "Key" but...
My ancestors fought to endure circumstances that threatened to hinder their elevation like Black Codes. I similarly fought to extricate myself from codes imposed on me by my undesired environment. I am grateful that I was able to be exposed to other cultures and codes by way of travel and education. But as I become an advocate of

the institution that freed me. I am being exposed to its flaws.

If one asks the question "Is public education in America providing the most adequate education to produce 21st Century student?" The answer is no in many regions. Even students in the well to do school districts feel somewhat unprepared for what is accepted as "the real world." If I can provide plausible strategies that could increase graduation rates, in a collaborative industry like education, someone is bound to listen and join into the conversation. I do understand that there are many external and environmental factors that hinder a child's education, but there are students that would be more engaged despite their circumstance if the delivery of education would relate to their survival. Or if there were adequately prepared teachers to instruct them.

Urban school districts and schools that serve socioeconomically disadvantaged students are mostly affected by poor teacher retention. It is imperative to identify and address these needs. The falling retention rates are causing major teacher shortages across the nation. With the impending shortage, many principals are caught in a scenario that forces them to hire a teacher that may not be sufficiently prepared to teach, but they are qualified to fill a needed position. Addressing the factors and effects with essential recruitment and retention strategies can help counteract the falling retention rates.

 America has written laws that define and govern the public education provided to millions of students every year. The current framework and curriculum still bear conspicuous initiatives put in place by our ancestral legislators. Traditional school follows a confirmative system that is often guarded by the cloak of tradition. These laws, initiatives, and traditions are marketed to optimally educate students in America and provide a voted reflection of law makers vantage point concerning student needs.

 As a nation, we collectively allot much time to current trends, controversies, and leisure. We have the luxury of scrolling our phones regardless of social class thanks to government supported cell phones and Wi-

Fi. We may be exposed to, but cannot truly empathize with citizens of other countries that are fighting every day for survival. We are guarded by freedom from tyrannical governments that control our livelihood.

We take for granted the one thing that people utilize to emancipate themselves from dire circumstances; education. While we settle for distractions and the industrial education system to guide our kids, other countries are manufacturing more socially, academically, and financially advanced students than us. Yet in many cases we have more resources readily available to our students, especially the under privileged students who are provided for by government funds.

Civilization is a word we don't use very often. It describes the most ancient form of people interacting and connecting to build a society. As a developed nation, we are on to words like "cities" and "country" to signify ancestral victories that claimed the territory we are familiar with. However, civilization is the epitome of what binds us as a global nation.

There are cars on the western and eastern hemispheres. There are computers and iPhones all over the world. Along with these products are technicians needed to maintenance them, and this creates an industry. Regardless of the geographical location. All schools do not suffer from the same problems, but if we broaden our perspectives and challenge education to interact more globally like other industries we could improve it. There may be solution to problems in America that have already been solved in China or vice versa.

One day in my history class, new students from a European country did not have to take a test, and this sparked the interest of native students. My co-teacher explained that they were not well versed in American History and would be allotted time to study first. As we progressed through the year I noticed that the foreign and native student became more engaged because they were able to swap genuinely dissimilar perspectives from their peers. This engagement naturally boosted assessment scores.

If we use our mediums of communication to exchange ideas and information with our peers around the world, teachers or students, it would enhance the way our children perceive the world and become better prepared for it no matter if they start on the inner or outer rings.

All of the above sounds great in theory. The reality is that people are in control of orchestrating the laws that govern people they cannot relate to. They are also not directly affected by the problems in education and society that call for great change. It is not to be mean, but if the principles in this book are applied to the people crying for change, the ones crying for the change would take personal responsibility for their own cause and change it.

I bide you good tidings.

About the Author

Toy Taylor is a native of Waco, Tx. She currently manages a behavior unit in Austin, Tx. For more information and other works by the author please visit toytaylorbooks.com.

Other Books:

A Peace of Edith

Publish 5 Books in 5 Months or Less

I have many other books!

Check out my site: toytaylorbooks.com

www.ingramcontent.com/pod-product-compliance
Lightning Source LLC
Chambersburg PA
CBHW031354040426
42444CB00005B/293